SONG OF INDIA

This title is part of a series of books entitled ESSENTIAL INDIA EDITIONS. Each book in the series will explore a foundational aspect of the country in new and thought-provoking ways.

~

ALSO IN THIS SERIES

SONG OF INDIA

A STUDY OF THE
NATIONAL ANTHEM

Rudrangshu Mukherjee

ALEPH

ALEPH

ALEPH BOOK COMPANY
An independent publishing firm
promoted by *Rupa Publications India*

First published in India in 2025
by Aleph Book Company
161-B/4, Gulmohar House,
Yusuf Sarai Community Centre,
New Delhi 110049

Copyright © Rudrangshu Mukherjee 2025

ISBN: 978-93-6523-845-7

1 3 5 7 9 10 8 6 4 2

For
Sharmila Tagore
a musical offering

CONTENTS

OVERTURE

$\mathcal{R}$abindranath Tagore is the author of the Indian national anthem, the subject of this book. Countless Indians across the world stand up in respect whenever the national anthem is played or sung. However, many of them do not even know who wrote the song. Even those who are aware of the authorship do not have adequate knowledge about the author, Rabindranath Tagore, his life and his creative genius. This chapter aims to provide a brief introduction to Rabindranath Tagore's life and work.

Rabindranath Tagore was born in Calcutta on 7 May 1861 and died in the same city on 7 August 1941. To those who do not know Bengali he is simply Tagore—an anglicized version of the old family name of Thakur. To almost all educated Bengalis he is just Rabindranath.

The Thakur family originally hailed from the district of Jessore, now in Bangladesh. One of Rabindranath Tagore's forefathers migrated to Calcutta in the beginning of the eighteenth century when the British had begun to establish a trading hub and settlement there. The story went that the family had lost its high-caste Brahmin status in Jessore because a member of the family had partaken of food with a Muslim. This loss of status made the family move to Calcutta where they came to live near fishermen on the banks of the river Hooghly. The poor fishermen needed Brahmins (even those who had lost their caste) for their ritual needs and they turned to this family and honoured them by calling them thakur (lord or master). Members of the family soon gave up their careers as priests and began to work as commercial agents of the English East India Company and through this avenue made enormous amounts of money. This fortune acquired legendary proportions under Rabindranath Tagore's grandfather, Dwarkanath Tagore (1794–1846), who was an entrepreneur, and had used his fortune, like many others in late eighteenth- and early nineteenth-century Calcutta, to buy landed estates in Bengal and Orissa. Dwarkanath was a close friend of Rammohun Roy (1772–1833), who pioneered the movement post 1815 to reform orthodox Hindu society and religious practices. Rabindranath Tagore's father, Debendranath (1817–1905), had a deep interest in India's spiritual and philosophical traditions and under his patriarchy the Tagore family mansion in Jorasanko (in north Calcutta) emerged as a major centre of cultural and literary activity in Calcutta. Rabindranath Tagore was the fourteenth child of his parents and like all his siblings showed musical and literary talent at a very young age.

Rabindranath had little or no formal education. At the age of twelve, his father took him to the hill station Dalhousie and opened up his mind to the world of nature, astronomy, Indian music, literature, and Indian philosophy. When he was only sixteen Rabindranath's first book of poems, *Kabikahini* (A Poet's Tale) was published. When he was sixteen his eldest brother, Dwijendranath (1840–1926)—mathematician, philosopher, and poet—brought out a literary journal called *Bharati* where Rabindranath published many pieces including essays on Dante and Petrarch whose works he had got to know in the library of his elder brother, Satyendranath (1842–1923), the first Indian to join the Indian Civil Service. In 1878, Rabindranath travelled to England to stay with Satyendranath and his wife Gyanadanandini. During his sojourn abroad for over a year, Rabindranath was exposed to Western ways of life and to Western music and literature. Some of the tunes and melodies that Rabindranath picked up in England were echoed in an opera, *Valmiki Prativa,* which he composed in 1881. In these various ways, Rabindranath's education was somewhat unique. He always remembered that there were ways to education that lay beyond the boundaries of the school walls. When, late in his life, he wrote about his childhood and growing up years, in a book called *Chhelebela* (Childhood), he remarked, 'I wandered around the outskirts of schools. House tutors were appointed and I played truant. Whatever I managed to get was from the proximity to human beings.'[1] By the time he entered his twenties, he was being recognized as a major poet in Bengali.

When he was around twenty-two years old, Rabindranath was asked by his father to look after the family estates. Rabindranath took this responsibility very seriously and after a period of training in the Estate's Offices in Calcutta, he went out into rural eastern Bengal where he travelled by boat as this was an area crisscrossed by rivers—the most important of which was the vast, ocean-like Padma. This journey of Rabindranath into the rural world had several momentous consequences for his intellectual and creative development.

---

[1] Rabindranath Tagore, *Chhelebela, Rabindra Rachanavali,* Vol. 11, Calcutta: Government of West Bengal, 1991, p. 119. Henceforth, *RR* (WB).

The first was that these travels brought him close to nature, a renewal and reaffirmation of the experiences that he had had as a boy at Dalhousie when he had walked among the woods and the hills and had watched the night sky with his father. In rural and riverine Bengal, his eyes, his senses, and his mind opened up to a different facet of nature. In a letter, dated June 1891, during one of his trips, he wrote:

> I cannot describe the wonderful moonlit nights I am now having here. It is not my purpose to say that the address where this letter will reach does not witness moonlit nights—there over the maidan, over the church spire and over the silent trees the moonlight establishes its quiet presence.... Here I have nothing but the silent night. I won't be able to express the infinite peace and beauty I experience all by myself.... I put my head on the window sill, the wind caresses my hair, the river gurgles on, the moonlight shimmers and often the eyes are filled with tears.[2]

The second was that from the boat and on the ground, he observed the lives of the common people—the grinding poverty that dominated their lives, their daily routine,

---

[2]Rabindranath Tagore, *Chhinnapatra*, *RR* (WB), Vol. 11, 1991, p. 313.

their rituals, their ceremonies, their festivals, and their entertainments. In another letter, he wrote:

> The current of life in the village is not very swift, nor is it altogether sluggish or choked up. Work and rest seem to go hand in hand. The ferry-boat plying from one bank to another; the passers-by walking, umbrella in hand, along the bank of the canal; the women dipping their wicker-baskets in the water to wash the rice; the peasants making for the market with bundles of jute on their heads; two men cutting up the fallen trunk of a tree with loud strokes of their axes; a carpenter, tool in hand, repairing a boat he has turned upside down in the shade of an *aswattha* tree; the village dog loitering aimlessly by the side of the canal; a number of cows, their bellies full of the luxuriant monsoon grass, lying in the sun and idly flapping their ears or wriggling their tails to keep off the flies and, when the crows sitting on the ridge of their spines annoy them too much, bending their heads back to signify their objection. The few monotonous sounds of tapping and knocking that one hears here, the noises of children at play, the high wailing notes of the herdsman's song, the splash of oars,

the groaning of the oil-presses, are in perfect tune
with the twitter of birds and the murmur of leaves.
They all seem to be part of a quiet, dreamy, tender
symphony—elaborate yet restrained.[3]

He discovered how the rhythm of everyday life served as
the means of sustenance for the common people in spite
of the exploitation and the poverty that engulfed their
lives. In his mind, he could fuse together his closeness to
nature and his observations of the lives of poor people.
In another letter, dated 10 May 1893, he expressed this
coming together in a very moving way: 'I see now large,
swollen clouds have gathered all around...here the play of
sunshine and clouds is so important—how people stare
at the sky.... I feel very sad and compassionate seeing
my poor peasant subjects. They are like the Almighty's
helpless children. They have nothing unless the Almighty
gives it to them. When the earth's milk dries up, they only
know how to cry—when their hunger is assuaged, they
forget everything.'[4]

    This exposure to nature and the rural world found
expression in a series of outstanding short stories,

[3]Quoted in Somnath Maitra, 'Letters of Rabindranath Tagore' in
Rabindranath Tagore 1861-1961: A Centenary Volume, New Delhi: Sahitya
Akademi, 1961, p. 164.
[4]Rabindranath Tagore, *Chchinnapatra*, RR (WB), Vol. 11, pp. 346–47.

which were published in the mid-1890s as *Galpaguccha* (Collection of Stories), and also in many memorable songs and poems. But there was an equally important fallout. The sufferings of human beings that he saw first-hand touched him profoundly. In an unforgettable poem written in 1894, Rabindranath wrote: 'There standing bowed head and dumb on their downcast faces written only the story of hundred years of pain and sorrow. Greater the burden on their shoulders, they move slowly as long as they have life—then they bequeath the burden to their children generation after generation. They do not display their anger at destiny, they do not abuse the gods, they do not blame humankind, they harbour no umbrage, for their painful lives they eke out only a few grains of rice.'[5]

This suffering brought to him new commitment which he expressed in a prayer-like poem, published in 1901: 'Give me the strength never to disown the poor or bend my knees before insolent might.'[6] His commitment to the poor was lifelong. He was to write in 1916, 'Man's

[5]Rabindranath Tagore, 'Ebar Phirao More', *RR* (WB), Vol. 2, pp. 141–44.
[6]Rabindranath Tagore, 'Naibedya', *Rabindra Rachanavali*, Viswa Bharati, Vol. 4, p. 312. Henceforth *RR*, (VB). I take the translation from France Bhattacharya, 'Rabindranath, Bhakti and the Bhakti Poets', in Sukanta Chaudhuri (ed.), *The Cambridge Companion to Rabindranath Tagore*, Cambridge: Cambridge University Press, 2020, p. 388.

history is waiting in patience for the triumph of the insulted man.'[7]

From the time he began touring parts of the Bengal countryside to look after his family's landed estates, he became concerned and then involved with the welfare of the people who lived in the villages. He wrote about their problems in his essays. Later on, he devoted himself to the welfare and development of villages around Santiniketan. Rabindranath's concern and dedication to service to the poor were also reflected in his creative work—especially his short stories and in some of his novels.

The experience of witnessing the lives of the poor had a profound impact on Rabindranath's view of history. In the early twentieth century, he wrote that the wars and hunts of kings did not affect in any way the ways in which the lives of the rural poor were organized. He invoked the same idea with greater clarity in an essay entitled 'Sahitye Aitihasikata' (Historicality in Literature), written in May 1941. Towards the end of that essay, he went back to his travels in the countryside of Bengal and wrote:

---

[7]Rabindranath Tagore, 'Stray Birds #317' in Sisir Kumar Das (ed.), *The English Writings of Rabindranath Tagore*, 3 vols, New Delhi: Sahitya Akademi, 1994–96, Vol. 1, p. 434.

Once when I used to travel by boat along the rivers of Bengal and came to sense its playful vitality, my inner soul delighted in gathering those wonderful impressions of weal and woe in my heart which were composed into sketches of country life month after month.... There is no doubt that the rural scenes surveyed by the poet in those days were affected by the conflicts of political history. However, what came to be reflected in *Galpaguccha* was not the image of a feudal order nor indeed any political order at all, but the history of the weal and woe of human life which with its everyday contentment and misery, has always been there in the peasants' fields and village festivals, manifesting their simple and abiding humanity across all of history—sometimes under Mughal rule, sometimes under British rule. I am not acquainted with at least three-quarters of that far-flung history in which the critics of today wander about so extensively. That is why I guess it upsets me so much. I have in my mind to say, 'Off with your history'.[8]

---

[8]Rabindranath Tagore, 'Historicality in Literature' in Rudrangshu Mukherjee (ed.), *The Best of Tagore*, London: Everyman's Library, 2023, p. 652. The translation is by Ranajit Guha.

History, for Rabindranath, was in the rhythms of the quotidian.

History, or the history that Rabindranath would come to loathe and reject, impinged on his life in a very significant way at the beginning of the twentieth century. In 1904–05, history pulled him to a different direction. The then viceroy, Lord Curzon, announced that from October 1905, Bengal would be partitioned into two provinces. The official reason given was that of administrative expediency. But the real reason was to separate Bengal into a Hindu-majority part and a Muslim-majority part, so that Hindus and Muslims could not come together to oppose British rule. Rabindranath, together with other members of the Bengali intelligentsia were steadfastly opposed to this proposal to divide Bengal and the Bengalis. On 16 October 1905—Partition Day on which Calcutta observed a hartal—a gathering of people, including Rabindranath who was at the forefront, went to the river Hooghly and started the day with a dip in the river. After this, they tied rakhis on each other's wrists. On the same day, he was present at two very large public meetings. He lent his support to build a national fund. On the very first day of the launch of the fund ₹30,000 was raised. In the course of his involvement with this anti-partition movement, Rabindranath composed a number of memorable patriotic songs. Among these were 'Amar Sonar Bangla' (My Golden Bengal) which was to become, in 1971, the national anthem of Bangladesh, and 'Jadi Tor Dak Shune Keu Na Ashe Tobe Ekla Cholo Re' (If no one listens to your call, then walk alone) which became one of Mahatma Gandhi's favourite songs.[9]

One of the key elements in the movement was the idea of swadeshi—the boycott of foreign goods and the use of Indian ones. Rabindranath championed this idea. But he went a step further. He wrote: 'The salt from Liverpool and the cloth from Manchester do not harm us so much. But voluntarily accepting foreign customs and getting tied to them distorts our mind.... The last fortress of our freedom is our heart—the key to that is in our own hands, the king does not have the strength to enter there. If we ourselves allow foreign customs to work there, then we will be reduced to the plight of beggars and gain the humiliation of slaves.'[10]

As the movement gained momentum what dismayed Rabindranath was the deployment of coercion in the

---

[9]For the Swadeshi Movement, see Sumit Sarkar, *The Swadeshi Movement in Bengal, 1903-1908*, Ranikhet: Permanent Black, 2010. Also see, Rudrangshu Mukherjee, *Tagore and Gandhi: Walking Alone, Walking Together*, New Delhi: Aleph Book Company, 2021.
[10]Mukherjee, *Tagore and Gandhi*, p. 8.

enforcement of boycott. He wrote about the various ways through which the boycott was being imposed on those who refused to obey the boycott call—from the threat that their forefathers would rot in hell, to the stoppage of essential services like the barber, washerman, etc., to the burning of houses and thrashing people in public. He emphasized that the main victims of such acts of coercion were invariably the poor and members of the lower classes whose interests and advantages the movement had sought to suppress. Boycott, Rabindranath argued, was dividing the people because it was being imposed and was therefore not based on voluntary consent. He raised the ethical question of ends and means and pointed out that something noble and good could not be accomplished by force and violence. His growing disillusionment made him turn away from the movement and focus on village reconstruction.

In 1906–07, he had spoken about the need to start from what he called 'village patriotism'. At the heart of this was the welfare of the villages—education, cleaning the ponds, building roads, preventing the oppression of the weak in the hands of the strong. All these had to be seen as the responsibility of the people themselves and not as things that were to be carried out by external agencies like the state. He practised what he preached and he began the project of village reconstruction in his own landed estates. The outcome of his efforts was considerable—three free health centres, more than two hundred primary schools, as well as night schools for adults, numerous public works, and a rural bank to fight moneylenders.[11] It was this very close exposure to rural life—unlike watching it from a boat as he had done in the 1890s—that led to a disillusionment of a different kind. He expressed this in a letter written in July 1908: he became critical of the way the caste-ridden Hindu society functioned. The prayer-like poem quoted earlier ('Give me the strength never to disown the poor....') began to acquire a salience in Rabindranath's activities. He became acutely conscious of the parasitical position of the zamindar. To his son-in-law, Nagendranath Gangopadhyay, who he had sent abroad along with his own son, Rathindranath, to study agricultural science, Rabindranath wrote on 29 October 1907: 'Remember that the landlord's wealth is actually the peasants: they are bearing the cost of your education by starving or half-starving themselves. It is your responsibility to repay this debt in full. That is your first task, even

---

[11]Sarkar, *The Swadeshi Movement in Bengal, 1903–1908*, 2010, p. 10.

before the welfare of your own family.'[12]

Apart from village reconstruction, the other area to which Rabindranath devoted his attention was education. In 1862, Debendranath had bought some property in Bolpur in the district of Birbhum in West Bengal. Debendranath had handed over the property to a board of trustees and had specified in the trust deed that the space was to be used for meditation on the supreme formless being. On the property had been established a temple of worship, a site for prayer and dwelling place called Santiniketan (the abode of peace). Rabindranath decided to start an experimental education institution in Santiniketan—a school that would not be like the conventional school but would be modelled on the forest hermitages of ancient India. Pointing out where his 'school' departed from others, Rabindranath wrote: 'From our very childhood, habits are formed and knowledge is imparted in such a manner that our life is weaned away from nature and our mind and the world are set in opposition from the beginning of our days. Thus the greatest of educations for which we come prepared is neglected, and we are made to lose

---

[12]Sankha Ghosh, 'Rabindranath Tagore: From Art to Life', Chaudhuri (ed.), *The Cambridge Companion to Rabindranath Tagore*, pp. 7–8.

our world to find a bagful of information instead. We rob the child of his earth to teach him geography, of language to teach him grammar.'[13]

Within a few years, the school had grown and Rabindranath had also developed his own ideas of international co-operation. In tune with the latter, he added to his school in Santiniketan a new dimension. In 1921, he established a global university to which he gave the name, Visva Bharati. 'Yatra Visvam Bharati Ekanirham' (Where the World Makes Home in a Single Nest)—this was what Rabindranath made the motto of his educational institution.

In the villages around Santiniketan, Rabindranath pursued his project of village reconstruction and the welfare of the rural people. His aim was to structure the economy of these villages to make the people self-reliant in an environment whose principle would not be self-interest but co-operation. He wrote: 'The symptoms of our miseries cannot be removed from the outside, their causes must be extirpated from within. If we wish to do this, we must undertake two tasks; first, to educate everyone in the land, so as to unite them mentally with

---

[13]Kathleen M. O' Connell, 'Tagore's Santiniketan: Learning Associated with Life', Chaudhuri (ed.), *The Cambridge Companion to Rabindranath Tagore*, p. 297.

all the world...Secondly, to unite them among themselves in the sphere of their livelihood, so as to bring about their union with the world through their work.'[14]

Mention has just been made to Rabindranath's ideas of international co-operation. These ideas began to germinate in his mind when he began to travel across the world. He visited England in 1913. His aim was to see and understand the educational methods of the West. He also wanted people to know what he was trying to do in his school in Santiniketan. On this trip to England, he carried with him his own translations of some of his poems, mostly from *Gitanjali* (Song Offerings). He showed these translations to the painter William Rothenstein, who in turn showed them to the poet William Butler Yeats. After reading the translations, Yeats, while introducing the poems to a gathering of writers and intellectuals, made the following observation: 'I know of no man in my time who has done anything in the English language to equal these lyrics. Even as I read them in these literal English translations, they are exquisite in style and thought.'[15] That same year an English translation of *Gitanjali* was

---

[14]Sourin Bhattacharya, 'Tagore and Village Economy: A Vision of Wholeness', Chaudhuri (ed.), *The Cambridge Companion to Rabindranath Tagore*, p. 314.
[15]Mukherjee, *The Best of Tagore*, p. xvii.

published in England. The next year the Nobel Prize was awarded to Rabindranath, and two years later a knighthood was bestowed on him. Rabindranath was to remain a knight for a very short period. In 1919, following the massacre at Jallianwala Bagh in Amritsar—where on 13 April, Brigadier General Dyer fired into a peaceful crowd in an enclosed garden, killing and injuring hundreds— Rabindranath renounced his knighthood once the news of the massacre reached him. In his letter renouncing his knighthood, written at the end of May 1919 and addressed to Lord Chelmsford, the then Viceroy of India, Rabindranath described the massacre and the repressive measures that came in its aftermath as being 'without parallel in the history of civilised governments, barring some conspicuous exceptions, recent and remote'. He said the British empire in India possessed the 'most terribly efficient organisation for destruction of human lives....' Under these circumstances, Rabindranath continued, 'The time has come when badges of honour make our shame glaring in the incongruous context of humiliation, and I for my part wish to stand, shorn of all special distinctions, by the side of those of my countrymen, who, for their so-called insignificance, are liable to suffer degradation not fit for human beings. These are the reasons which have painfully compelled me to ask Your Excellency, with due reference and regret, to relieve me of my title of Knighthood....'[16]

Through the 1920s and 1930s, until age and ill health began to plague him, Rabindranath travelled within India and across the world—to the US, to Japan, to Europe, to Latin America, to China, and to Soviet Russia—spreading his message of universal humanism and international co-operation. His message of universal humanism went hand in hand with his rejection of nationalism and blind patriotism. As early as 1908, he had written to a friend that 'patriotism cannot be our final spiritual shelter'. He added, 'I will not buy glass for the price of diamonds, and I will never allow patriotism to triumph over humanity as long as I live. I took a few steps down that road and stopped: for when I cannot retain my faith in universal man standing over and above my country, when patriotic prejudices overshadow my God, I feel inwardly starved.'[17]

These travels in no way affected Rabindranath's creative activity. He continued to write poems, songs, novels, plays, and essays. He added in this period a new facet to his creativity. He began to paint.

---

[16]Ibid., p. xviii.
[17]Ibid.

Rabindranath had no formal training as a painter. Traces of his interest in visual expression can be located in the doodles he made in the margins of his manuscripts. These doodles over time began to acquire the shape of imaginary and grotesque figures. Instead of deleting words or sentences, Rabindranath would transform the cancellations or emendations into patterns or figures, and then sometimes he would string them together so that a page of a manuscript took on the shape of a drawing or an image. From such beginnings, Rabindranath took to painting—sometimes abstract, sometimes of plants and animals which did not exist in reality, landscapes, and often of women. His landscapes were almost always dark; his colours were earthy but many of his paintings, as Satyajit Ray, the film-maker, remarked, 'evoked...a joyous freedom'.[18] His paintings and drawings, uninfluenced by any artist, Western or Eastern, numbered over two thousand. They were utterly original.

In the last years of his life, his failing health in no way stopped Rabindranath's flow of creativity. Some of his most moving and profound poems were written in his last years.

Rabindranath's creative oeuvre and his work in other

---

[18]Satyajit Ray, 'Portrait of a Man', *UNESCO Courier*, December 1961.

spheres were diverse. On his seventy-fourth birthday he described his life as 'a garland of many Rabindranaths'. He himself said that he was a 'messenger of variety'.[19] He made lyric poetry the anchor of his creativity. In form, his poems ranged from Bengali verse-forms to sonnets and blank verse that he imbibed from Western literature and adapted for the Bengali language. Many of his later poems were composed in free verse. The themes of the poems were similarly varied: simple human concerns; love for/among human beings and devotional; some poems were political and full of satire; and there was humour and even nonsense. The moods of poems at times reflected the various seasons and moved seamlessly from the simple to the philosophically profound. In the words of Sukanta Chaudhuri, a leading authority on Rabindranath, the latter 'sets out to be the poet of everything there is, and succeeds in improbable measure in this impossible venture'.[20]

Much of Rabindranath's poetry was inextricably linked to his songs. He had no formal training in music. But he was born with an unerring ear, and before age

---

[19]Anisuzzaman, 'A Garland of Many Tagores', Chaudhuri (ed.), *The Cambridge Companion to Rabindranath Tagore*, pp. 12 and 20.
[20]Sukanta Chaudhuri, 'Tagore's Poetry: An Overview', Chaudhuri (ed.), *The Cambridge Companion to Rabindranath Tagore*, p. 80.

took its toll, a powerful and outstanding singing voice. His musical compositions were eclectic. He drew from Western tunes and ballads as well as from north Indian and Carnatic classical music, and from various different types of Bengali music-making—especially from the Bauls—wandering folk singers. Many of his songs were stirring, moving, and patriotic. His best songs were invariably touched by an ineffable poignancy. His love songs blurred the distinction between the profane and the sacred. There has been no lyricist and music-maker like him in the Bengali language.

Rabindranath's prose fiction consists of short stories, novels, and novellas. The immediate context of his short stories has already been discussed. Even before he had tried his hand at writing short stories, Rabindranath, when he was barely twenty, had written a novel, *Bauthakuranir Haat* (The Young Queen's Market). For Rabindranath, his prose fiction, like many other spheres of his creative endeavour, was a world of experimentation in form, in themes, and in narrative techniques.

In his novels he explored the world of domesticity and the complex web of human relationships embedded within the home and the family. One of the most remarkable features of his fictional world was Rabindranath's exploration and depiction of the lives of women—

their interiority, their anguish, the discrimination and neglect they suffered, and their strengths. In some ways, Rabindranath's own walks through what Umberto Eco has tellingly called 'the fictional woods' remained incomplete because he was forever experimenting with themes, form, and language.

The mention of language is important. Through his prose Rabindranath actually shaped and moulded the modern Bengali language. He built upon the legacy of Bankim Chandra Chattopadhyay (1838–94) but also broke from the latter's Sanskritized Bengali. Rabindranath was a self-conscious stylist, and his style never remained static. He broke from tradition and broke again and again from his own style. He refused to conform even with the standards he himself had set.

As World War II broke out and the world was engulfed in violence, Rabindranath wrote an address in Bengali for his eightieth birthday celebrations in 1941 in Santiniketan. He titled the speech 'Sabhyatar Sankat' (Crisis in Civilization)[21] and this is often and rightly considered his last testament. In this address, Rabindranath announced his complete disillusionment with Western civilization and its vehicle in India, British

---

[21]Mukherjee, *The Best of Tagore*, pp. 643–49.

rule. He admitted that his initial fascination for things British had grown out of his profound admiration for English literature. When he faced the reality that was India, he came to the realization that the standard-bearers of civilization could disown their standards when it suited their self-interest. The poverty of the people of India, the absence of basic amenities like food, clothes, water, education, and health made it evident that the so-called civilized race was contemptuously indifferent to the sufferings of millions of Indians. He was forced to admit to himself that in no other state with a modern administration had such neglect occurred. Rabindranath was no longer willing to describe British civilization as civilization.

In spite of this disillusionment and the ruin and devastation that he saw all around the world, Rabindranath refused to abandon hope. The address ended with a cry of hope as a last article of his creed: 'A day will come,' he wrote, 'when unvanquished Man will retrace his path of conquest, despite all barriers, to win back his lost human heritage.'

Rabindranath's faith in 'unvanquished Man' drew sustenance from the philosophy and the wisdom of the Upanishads from which he derived his sense of piety. But his faith and piety were not blind; they were capacious enough to admit questions and radical doubt. In 1926, as he witnessed religious riots, he wrote, 'Honest atheism is much better than this terrifying deluded religion.... I cannot see any solution except to burn all India's misguided religious faith in the flames of atheism and make an absolute fresh start.' In 1939, when he heard an account about a young girl who had been raped and murdered, he cried out: 'The godly faith of the scriptures scatters with the dust. The sky rings out: there is no escape, no redress.'[22]

The doubt was most starkly expressed in the poem 'Question' (1931). Addressing God he wrote, in era after era you have sent messengers who preached the message of love and forgiveness; at the end of the poem, he went on to ask God, 'Those who have made your air toxic, put out your light, have you forgiven them, have you loved them.'[23] The question unanswered—and unanswerable—constituted a radical doubt. Rabindranath lived with such unanswered questions to God. In one of his last poems written on 27 July 1941—composed ten days before his death—he posed yet again unanswerable questions:

---

[22]Chaudhuri, 'Tagore's Poetry: An Overview', *The Cambridge Companion to Tagore*, p. 73.
[23]Rabindranath Tagore, 'Prashna', *RR* (VB), Vol. 8, pp. 145–46.

The sun of the first day
Had asked the question
At the new emergence of Being
Who are you—
No answer was found
Years and years passed
The day's last sun
Uttered the last question on the shores of the
western sea
Who are you—
Did not get an answer.[24]

Perhaps, because of these doubts, he could describe, in his very last poem, life and creation to be deceptive but it was by enduring that deception, that one got to win the imperishable right to peace.[25]

〜

The song 'Jana Gana Mana' was composed in December 1911 during a remarkable phase of Rabindranath's multi-faceted creative evolution. But the song expresses

---

[24]Rabindranath Tagore, *Shesh Lekha*, #13, *RR*, (VB), Vol. 13, p. 124. The translation is mine.
[25]Ibid. I am using words and phrases from Supriya Chaudhuri's excellent translation in Sukanta Chaudhuri (ed.), *Rabindranath Tagore: Selected Poems*, New Delhi: Oxford University Press, 2004, p. 376.

very evocatively some of Rabindranath's abiding values and beliefs: his unswerving hope in humanity; his faith in a benign divinity that championed the destiny of India and Indians; and most importantly, his commitment to the unity of India and the harmonious existence of all Indians. It was the articulation of these values through music that made many Indian nationalist leaders choose 'Jana Gana Mana' as the national anthem of India.

HARMONY VARIATIONS

'The pealing anthem swells the note of praise'. This line from Thomas Gray's 'Elegy Written in a Country Churchyard' is an excellent definition of an anthem—it invariably is a song in praise. By extension, a national anthem of a nation state is a lyrical and stirring melody extolling the subject nation. Most national anthems have a halo of sacredness associated with the words and music. A national anthem is the identifying call of a nation state.

This last and important point was articulated by India's first prime minister, Jawaharlal Nehru, when he told the Constituent Assembly (Legislative) on 25 August 1948:

> The question of having a National Anthem tune to be played by orchestra and bands became an urgent one for us immediately after August 15, 1947. It was as important from the point of view of our Defence

Services and our foreign embassies and legations and other establishments. It was obviously not suitable for 'God Save the King' to be played by our army bands, or abroad, after the changeover to independence. We were constantly being asked as to what tune should be played on such occasions. We could not give an answer because the decision could only be made by the Constituent Assembly.

The 'Jana Gana Mana' tune, slightly varied, had been adopted as National Anthem by the Indian National Army in South-East Asia and had subsequently attained a degree of popularity in India also.

The matter came to a head on the occasion of the General Assembly of the United Nations in 1947 in New York. Our delegation was asked for our National Anthem for the orchestra to play on a particular occasion.[26]

Quite clearly, the General Assembly of the United Nations felt, as per the prevailing practice, to have a piece of music which could be identified with the new-born

---

[26]Statement by Jawaharlal Nehru on 25 August 1948 in response to a question raised by Kesava Rao. Quoted in *Constituent Assembly of India (Legislative) Debates*, Vol. 6, 1948, pp. 548–49.

Indian nation state. All nation states have national anthems, and they serve as one of the identifying symbols of the nation state together with the national flag. The flag and the anthem stand for the nation.

As noted, India's national anthem 'Jana Gana Mana' was a poem written and then set to music by Rabindranath Tagore in 1911. In the speech referred to above, Nehru added that the Indian delegation to the UN in New York had with them a record of 'Jana Gana Mana' and the delegation gave this to the orchestra who practised and played it. When the piece was played before a large gathering, it won applause and approbation. The tune struck them to be, in Nehru's words, 'distinctive and dignified'. This is perhaps the first occasion when 'Jana Gana Mana' was played in an international forum as India's song, even though it still had not been adopted as the national anthem of India by the Constituent Assembly. Nehru had emphasized that *only* the Constituent Assembly could decide which piece of music/song would be India's national anthem.

The formal announcement that 'Jana Gana Mana' would be the national anthem of India was made by President Rajendra Prasad to the Constituent Assembly when it met for the last time on 24 January 1950 to sign the Constitution of India. Rajendra Prasad said:

There is one matter which has been pending for discussion, namely, the question of the National Anthem. At one time it was thought that the matter might be brought up before the House and a decision taken by the House by way of a resolution. But it has been felt that instead of taking a formal decision by means of a resolution it was better if I make a statement with regard to the National Anthem. Accordingly, I make this statement—'The composition consisting of the words and music known as *Janaganamana* is the National Anthem of India subject to such alteration in the words as Government may authorise as occasion arises; and the song *Varde Mataram* which has played a historic part in the struggle for freedom shall be honoured equally with *Janaganamana* and shall have equal status with it'.[27]

Once the signing of the Constitution was over, a member, Ananthasayanam Ayyangar, requested that the assembled members should collectively sing 'Jana Gana Mana'. The president gave his consent. Members of the Constituent Assembly, including the president, sang 'Jana Gana Mana' in chorus which was led by Purnima Banerjee (one of the

---

[27] *Constituent Assembly Debates*, Vol. 12, [online facsimile], pp. 255, 258.

fifteen women members of the Constituent Assembly).[28]
It could be said that this was the formal debut of 'Jana
Gana Mana' as the national anthem of India.

At the risk of digressing a little bit, two rather
significant points need to be noted. One is what Nehru
wrote regarding India's national anthem in the centenary
year of Tagore's birth. While penning a moving tribute
to the poet and his many-splendored creativity and
personality, Nehru wrote:

> During my last visit to him I requested him to
> compose a National Anthem for the new India.
> He partly agreed. At that time I did not have 'Jana
> Gana Mana', our present national anthem, in
> mind. He died soon after. It was a great happiness
> to me when some years later after the coming of
> Independence, we adopted 'Jana Gana Mana' as
> our National Anthem. I have a feeling of satisfaction
> that I was partly responsible for this choice, not
> only because it is a great national song, but also
> because it is a constant reminder to all our people
> of Rabindranath Tagore.[29]

---

[28]Ibid.
[29]'On Rabindranath Tagore', Madhavan K. Palat (ed.), *Selected Works
of Jawaharlal Nehru*, Second Series, Vol. 69, New Delhi: Jawaharlal
Nehru Memorial Library, 2016, p. 508. This piece first appeared as an

The second is how Subhas Chandra Bose, in exile from India in the early 1940s, adopted 'Jana Gana Mana' as the national anthem. When Bose inaugurated the Free India Centre in Europe on 2 November 1942, the song was chosen by him as the national anthem—this predated by eight years the official acceptance of the song as the national anthem of the Indian republic. Under Bose's leadership, a Hindustani version of the song was made the national anthem. This version was rendered by Abid Hasan, and Mumtaz Hussain composed the song in three verses. Ram Singh Thakur made a score for bands to play based on the original tune.[30]

It is noteworthy that two outstanding patriots— Nehru and Bose—roughly around the same time, were thinking of a national anthem for a new and independent India. Bose in 1942 had already adopted 'Jana Gana Mana' as the national anthem; and Nehru in his last meeting with Tagore, shortly before the latter's death in 1941, had requested the poet to compose a national anthem. It is obvious that both Nehru and Bose were

---

Introduction to *Rabindranath Tagore 1861-1961: A Centenary Volume*, New Delhi: Sahitya Akademi, 1961, p. xvi.

[30]I take these details from Sugata Bose, 'Our National Anthem', *The Nation as Mother and Other Visions of Nationhood*, New Delhi: Viking, 2017, pp. 168–69.

confident that an India free from British rule was
no longer a distant dream but lay in the immediate
future.

ſ

The story of its composition and of its first singing should
be recollected. In 1937, Pulinbihari Sen, a close associate
of Tagore, wrote to him enquiring about the context for
the song. Tagore replied:

> Someone well-placed in government circles
> who was a friend of mine specially requested
> me to compose a song in praise of the Emperor
> [George V]. I was amazed at this request
> and the amazement was laced with anger. It
> was as a strong reaction and opposition to
> this request that I proclaimed the victory of
> the champion of India's destiny in the song
> Janaganamana adhinayaka; this champion is the
> eternal charioteer is the guide of the travellers
> on the hazardous path of rise and fall and is in
> the hearts of the multitude and their guide. That
> such an eternal charioteer of humanity's destiny
> cannot be George V or VI or any other George
> was perceived by my loyalist friend because

despite his devotion [to the Emperor] he was not
bereft of intelligence.[31]

There is some speculation, if not a puzzle, regarding
the identity of this loyalist friend. In a book on India's
national anthem, Prabodhchandra Sen suggested that
possibly Ashutosh Chaudhuri was the friend.[32] But
when Sen wrote an English version of the book[33], he
made no mention of Chaudhuri as being the person
who had made the request to Tagore and, in fact, did
not identify the friend. This erasure is something of a
mystery. Was it because in the one year that separated
the Bengali and the English book, he had discovered that
his identification had been wrong, or was it because he
thought that Ashutosh Chaudhuri would be too obscure
a person for non-Bengali readers?

The mystery deepens because Prasantakumar Pal,

---

[31]Tagore to Pulinbihari Sen, 20 November 1937, Prasantakumar Pal,
Rabijibani, Vol. 6, Calcutta: Ananda Publishers, 1993, p. 256n140. The
translation is mine.
[32]Prabodhchandra Sen, *Bharatbarsher Jatiya Sangeet*, Calcutta: Purbasha,
1948, p. 2n1. Ashutosh Chaudhuri (1860–1924) was a very close friend of
Tagore and was married to his niece. He was a very successful barrister-
at-law and was appointed a judge of the Calcutta High Court. He belonged
to the Moderate section of the Indian National Congress and was active in
the Swadeshi Movement. He was knighted in 1921.
[33]Prabodhchandra Sen, *India's National Anthem*, Calcutta: Visva Bharati,
1949.

who wrote a very detailed multi-volume (but unfinished) biography of Tagore, thought that Prabodhchandra Sen had been wrong in identifying Chaudhuri as the friend Tagore had written about. He went to argue that it was much more justified to identify Prodyut Kumar Tagore as the concerned friend. Prodyut Tagore's loyalism was so pronounced that he was one of the two persons who had held the state umbrella as the King and the Queen had walked to the pageant that had been organized in Calcutta in their honour.[34] Pal was only making an educated guess. In the absence of hard evidence, the identity of the friend Tagore had referred to remains shrouded in obscurity.

What is crystal clear, however, is that Tagore did not write 'Jana Gana Mana' in praise of George V. 'Jana Gana Mana' was first sung on the second day (27 December) of the 1911 session of the Indian National Congress held in Calcutta. Both Jnananjan Niyogi and Nilratan Sircar were involved in the arrangements and organization of this session. At Sircar's request, Niyogi got the song from Tagore and gave it to Sircar. Before it was sung

---

[34]Pal, *Rabijibani*, Vol. 6, p. 256. Prodyutkumar Tagore (1873–1942) belonged to the Pathuriaghata branch of the Tagore family. He was the first Indian to become a member of the Royal Photography Society. He was knighted in 1906 and given the title maharaja in 1908.

in the Congress session, rehearsals were held at Sircar's house on Harrison Road in Calcutta.[35]

It is important to sketch the context for this session of the Congress. One important section of the Congress in this period was labelled the Moderates, led at this time by Surendranath Banerjee. A few days before the Congress session in Delhi, George V had revoked the partition of Bengal which, as we have seen, had happened in 1905, following a decision taken during the viceroyalty of Lord Curzon. The partition had provoked the Swadeshi Movement (1905–08), a major political movement in Bengal—demonstrations, protest meetings, boycott of foreign goods, displays of Hindu–Muslim unity, a cultural efflorescence, and even violence towards the end of the movement. Repression to end the movement was severe. The government used arrests, preventive detention, deportation, and press censorship.[36] Tagore had been at the forefront of the Swadeshi Movement till its violent phase. In the

---

[35]Sen, *Bharatbarsher Jatiya Sangeet*, p. 5n3. Jnananjan Niyogi (1891–1956) was a freedom fighter and social reformer, very well known in Bengal. Nilratan Sircar (1861–1943) was an exact contemporary and close friend of Tagore. He was an eminent doctor, philanthropist, and swadeshi entrepreneur.

[36]For details of this movement, see Sumit Sarkar, *The Swadeshi Movement in Bengal, 1903-1908*, Ranikhet: Permanent Black, 2010.

course of his participation in the Swadeshi Movement, Tagore had made his patriotism and his sentiments against British rule abundantly clear.[37] Some of his most powerful and stirring patriotic songs were composed during this phase of his life. Commenting on Tagore's creativity during this period, Ezra Pound was to write later, 'Tagore has sung Bengal into a nation'.[38]

King George V and others in the higher echelons of power in London acknowledged that the partition had not been a wise and tactical move. The king wanted to revoke the partition and intended to do so at the Coronation Durbar which he was determined to hold in India.

The king's visit to India—the first by a British monarch—took place in the winter of 1911, and the grand durbar began with the state entry into Delhi of the king and the queen. At the very end of the durbar, the king snatched a paper from the hands of the viceroy, Lord Hardinge, and read out the announcement of the change of capital from Calcutta to Delhi and to revoke

---

[37]For Tagore's participation in the Swadeshi Movement and his withdrawal from it, see Mukherjee, *Tagore and Gandhi*, pp. 1–45.
[38]Quoted in S. Gopal, *British Policy in India: 1858-1905*, Cambridge: Cambridge University Press, 1965, p. 274.

the partition of Bengal.[39] While the shifting of the capital caused great dismay among the British population in Calcutta, the annulment of the partition brought much delight to some Bengalis, especially those belonging to the Moderate section of the Congress. An incident after the conclusion of the durbar was the subject of first bewilderment and then mirth. As the crowd was dispersing from the amphitheatre, some bare-headed people were seen approaching the dais and bending themselves double before the thrones. It seemed from their gestures that they had raised the royal couple to the level of Hindu deities to whom they were offering worship. It was discovered that these people were Bengalis making an exhibition of their loyalty to the king and queen and thus to the Raj.[40]

The Moderates decided that the best occasion to demonstrate their loyalty to the king would be at the Congress session in Calcutta, especially as the royal couple was scheduled to visit Calcutta on 30 December, two days after the conclusion of the Congress session. To show their loyalty, the Moderates needed a song in

[39]For a description of the durbar, see Rudrangshu Mukherjee, 'Old Seat for a New Empire: Calcutta to Delhi', Malvika Singh and Rudrangshu Mukherjee, *New Delhi: Making of a Capital*, New Delhi: Roli Books, 2011.
[40]Ibid., p. 26.

praise of the king. It is possible that Tagore's loyalist friend (whoever he was) had approached the poet to write such a song. When Tagore refused, the Moderates had to look elsewhere for a song in praise of the king.

The Congress session was inaugurated by the singing of 'Vande Mataram'. The proceedings of the second day began with the singing of 'Jana Gana Mana'. After this some letters and telegrams were read out and a proposal welcoming the royal couple and expressing loyalty to them was presented. After this proposal was accepted a song of praise of the royal couple in Hindi was sung. It is possible that the Moderates had found this song or had had this song composed after Tagore's refusal. Surendranath Banerjee's journal *The Bengalee* in its report made a clear distinction between the two songs: 'The proceedings commenced with a patriotic song composed by Babu Rabindranath Tagore, the leading poet of Bengal...then a Hindi song paying heartfelt homage to Their Imperial Majesties was sung by the Bengali boys and girls in chorus.'[41] The nationalist daily *Amrita Bazar Patrika* made a similar distinction calling 'Jana Gana Mana' 'a Bengali song of benediction' and the Hindi song as a 'song in honour of Their Imperial Majesties

---

[41]Surendranath Banerjee (ed.), *The Bengalee*, 28 December 1911.

visit to India'.[42] The official report of the Congress for this session described Tagore's composition as 'a patriotic song' and the Hindi one as 'a song of welcome to Their Imperial Majesties....'[43] It should be noted, however, that *The Englishman* and *The Statesman*—both considered the vehicles of white and imperial opinion—made no such distinction. Both described Tagore's song as being a 'song' (*The Englishman*) and a 'hymn' (*The Statesman*) of welcome to the king-emperor. [44]

The proceedings of the third day began with the song 'Atita-Gaurava-vahini mama vani gaha aji Hindustan', which was also known by the name 'Namo Hindustan'. This song was written by Sarala Devi (1872–1945), Tagore's niece, and had been sung in the 1901 session of the Congress held in Calcutta.[45] Thus, it is obvious that singing of songs during Congress sessions was an established practice. In the winter of 1886, Tagore was persuaded by his friend Tarak Nath Palit to attend the second session of the Congress in Calcutta. Tagore attended but somewhat disenchanted by the mendicancy of the Congress, he sang, when requested to sing, his

---

[42]*Amrita Bazar Patrika*, 28 December 1911.
[43]Sen, *India's National Anthem*, p. 9.
[44]*The Englishman*, 28 December 1911; *The Statesman*, 28 December 1911.
[45]Sen, *Bharatbarsher Jatiya Sangeet*, p. 7.

own composition, 'Amaye bolo na gahita' (Do not ask me to sing). This dampened the celebratory mood of the gathering. Again, after the conclusion of the 1890 session, there was a reception for the volunteers in early January 1891, and there, Tagore sang 'Jaye Bharater jay, gao Bharater Jay'.[46] In 1911, two old and well-known songs were sung—'Vande Mataram' and 'Namo Hindustan'—as well two new ones—'Jana Gana Mana' and a Hindi song of praise to welcome the royal couple.

In January 1912, one month after the singing of 'Jana Gana Mana' in the Congress session, the text of the song was published in the *Tattvabodhini Patrika* of which Tagore was the editor. This journal was the mouthpiece of the Adi Brahmo Samaj. The text was published under the rubric Brahmo sangeet. This made it clear that the song was not in praise of any individual, living or dead. On 25 January, in the Tagore household, on the occasion of Maghotsava (a ceremony very special and auspicious to the members of the Brahmo Samaj), 'Jana Gana Mana' was sung under the direction of Tagore himself. The musical notation (swaralipi) of this song was done by Dinendranath Tagore (1882–1935), who was the grandson of Tagore's eldest brother, Dwijendranath. It

---

[46]Mukherjee, *Tagore and Gandhi*, pp. xv and 1.

was noted that the song bore the influence of the raga Iman and the tala was Kaharba.[47]

Having presented the context of the song and its composition, it is necessary to turn to the text of the song. It is important to underline that only the first verse of this rather longish song, consisting of five verses, forms the national anthem of India. The entire song is printed in this book—in the Bengali script, in the Devanagiri script, in the Roman script, and Tagore's own English translations of the song.[48]

The song begins by hailing the dispenser of India's destiny who is the captain of the minds of people. It proceeds to delineate the geography of India in terms of

---

[47]These details regarding the swaralipi and influence of Iman and the tala are taken from Purnendu Bikash Sarkar (ed. and comp.), *Rabindranath Thakur: Gitabitan Tathyabhandar*, Calcutta: Signet Press, 2019.

[48]One of Tagore's translations of the song is taken from Sisir Kumar Das (ed.), *The English Writings of Rabindranath Tagore*, Vol. 1, New Delhi: Sahitya Akademi, 1994. It is reprinted in Mukherjee, *The Best of Tagore*, pp. 677–78. Tagore also made another translation, a facsimile of which is printed in this book. To this translation he gave the title 'The Morning Song of India'. This translation was done in 1919, when he spent five days at the Theosophical College, Madanapalle, at the invitation of the principal, James Cousins. There he sang 'Jana Gana Mana', and at the request of the audience, he made the translation. See, Sen, *India's National Anthem*, p. 23.

the various regions of India, its mountain ranges and its rivers—over this entire geographical expanse the name of this dispenser of destiny rises, prays for blessings, and sings of victory. The end of the first verse introduces the refrain, 'Jaye hey' (victory), reiterated many times at the end of each verse. The first verse makes it clear that this is a song for India and India's history and destiny.

The second verse is about India's demographic plurality and the many religious faiths that coexist in India. The poet mentions Hindus, Buddhists, Sikhs, Jains, Parsis, Muslims, and Christians. Every day this message of tolerance is heard, and the people of many faiths, from the east and the west, gather around the throne of the dispenser of India's destiny and string a garland of love. The people are one and united. The idea of unity in diversity which had already become a part of the discourse of the nationalist movement in India is invoked by Tagore in no uncertain terms.

The third verse is about history: its hazardous path traversed by people over epochs marking their rise and fall. The dispenser of destiny is now described as an everlasting charioteer, the wheels of whose chariot guide human beings through the trials of revolution and the sounds of whose conch shell resound with hope amidst crisis and despair. The charioteer is the one who has shown the path. Tagore was obviously referring to the many changes that India's history had witnessed but also suggesting that through all the tribulations of change, there has been a beacon of continuity.

Continuing on the register of history and change within continuity, the words continue to speak of the periods of impenetrable darkness of night when the country seemed to have lost its consciousness, but the dispenser of destiny was ever awake and unflinchingly steadfast. Thus, the tender mother, the poet affirms, acted as the saviour during times of terror and fear. The dispenser of destiny is the saviour of the people from sorrow and suffering. History has been a long night of darkness.

But the night has ended, as the sun rises in the eastern hills. There is a promise of a new life in the wind and the music of the birds. Nurtured by the mother's compassion, sleeping India awakes with its head at her feet. There is a significant alteration in the refrain. All the previous verses had dispenser of India's destiny (Bharata bhagya bidhata), but in the final verse the phrase, the dispenser of India's destiny is preceded by rajeswar—king of kings.

Even from this bald summary of a very evocative song, some points emerge that need to be highlighted.

The most obvious is Tagore's firm belief—almost an article of faith—that there is some entity—dispenser of India's destiny, Bharata bhagya bidhata, eternal charioteer, he uses different epithets—that is in command of India's destiny. It is with this entity's auspicious blessings that India and Indians navigate the 'many cunning passages, contrived corridors' that history has (to use T. S. Eliot's phrase in 'Gerontion'). This belief was an integral part of Tagore's piety. He was a devout man but his piety was not devoid of doubt, as we have noted in the previous chapter. This song, however, has not even a hint of a doubt about the existence and the role of the eternal and divine guiding hand. This song is an ode to that Being.

The song is also about what can be called—for the lack of a better phrase—the spirit or the idea of India. This is an India that is geographically vast, encompassing a range of natural features—from mountains to rivers to regions. It is an India in which many different kinds of people live in harmony. The differences are not just regional but also of religious faith. Yet they all live together and in unison sing in praise of Bharata bhagya bidhata. This harmony and unity willed by the Eternal Being shapes the spirit/idea of India. There was no doubt in Tagore's mind about the oneness and the unity of India. It is significant that in two places in the song, he used 'necklace of love' (premahara) and 'music of compassion' (karunaraga) in the context of his idealization of the Eternal Being that drives India. Such an Eternal Being can only be extolled, and Tagore does so again and again at the end of every verse.

It is worth pausing on the word rajeswar (king of kings or king of iswara, God) which Tagore inserted in the last refrain. A year before he wrote 'Jana Gana Mana', Tagore had written a play called *Raja* (literally King, but the play is translated as *King of the Dark Chamber*) in which the king never appears on stage but is only heard by his bewildered queen, Sudarshana, and her companion, Surangama, who is devoted to the king. In the second scene of the play, Tagore introduced a song whose first line goes (in rough translation) like this, 'We are all king in the kingdom of our king'. Where everyone is king, there is no need for the physical presence of a king: he is invisible, inhabiting the chambers of everyone's heart. Tagore was celebrating a unique notion of sovereignty—a notion captured by the word rajeswar. He hailed the victory of the rajeswar in every sovereign individual's heart and consciousness. There is a gesture here towards popular sovereignty—a realm where everyone is a king.

India's past, present, and future are both integral parts of the later strophes of the song. The past is described as a long and dark night when the country was

oppressed, exploited, and bereft of consciousness. The
question that inevitably arises is, did Tagore consider the
entire past of India to be dark and without the light of
consciousness? Or was he implying that the immediate
past—India under British rule—was an era under the
looming shadows of gloom and despair? The lines that
follow about the dawn of a new India would suggest
that he was referring to the immediate past. A sleeping
India is awakening to a new future.

The identity of the divine dispenser—bhagya bidhata—
is ungendered. Though it could be argued with some
justification that the use of the word adhinayaka (captain)
can be taken as indicative of a male presence. But any
uncertainty in the readers'/listeners' minds is dispelled
in the penultimate stanza where this Being is described
as the tender and compassionate mother. When Tagore
composed this song, the visualization of the nation as the
mother had become part of the nationalist discourse—
in fiction, in discursive prose, and more emphatically,
in poetry and song.[49] Tagore himself, during his active
participation in the Swadeshi Movement in 1905–06,

---

[49]For a perceptive and critical analysis of this depiction of the nation as
mother, see Tanika Sarkar, 'Nationalist Iconography: Image of Women
in 19th century Bengali Literature', *Economic and Political Weekly*, 21
November 1987.

had written songs in which he had identified Bengal as
the mother and motherland. The idea harked back most
memorably to Bankim Chandra Chattopadhyay. In his
famous novel, *Anandamath* (1882), Bankim Chandra had
included his poem 'Vande Mataram' (written in 1875 to
fill a blank page in his journal *Bangadarshan*). The poem
had been set to music by Tagore and sung by him for
the first time in public in the 1896 session of the Indian
National Congress held in Calcutta.[50] It was written
explicitly in praise of the motherland which in the poem
is identified with Bengal. One of the early identifications
of Bharatvarsha as mother, at least in Bengali, occurs in
a song by another famous literary figure, Dwijendralal
Roy (1863–1913), a contemporary of Tagore.[51] The nation
was also visually represented as mother, for example in
Abanindranath Tagore's painting *Bharatmata*.[52] The nation
was a source of nurturing and shelter just as a mother is

---

[50]These details are taken from Sugata Bose, 'The Nation as Mother' in his
The Nation as Mother, p. 3.

[51]Ibid., p. 4. The lines are 'Jedin sunil Jaladhi hotte uthile Janani
Bharatabarsha,/Shedin bishwe she ki kalarab, she ki ma bhakti, she ki ma
harsha.' (The day you arose from the blue ocean, Mother Bharavarsha,/
The world erupted in such joyful clamour, such devotion, Mother, and so
much laughter, Mother.) The translation is by Sugata Bose.

[52]The artist had initially entitled the painting Bangamata but later changed
it to Bharatmata. See, Tapati Guha-Thakurta, *The Making of a New 'Indian'
Art: Artist, Aesthetics and Nationalism in Bengal, c. 1850-1920*, Cambridge:
Cambridge University Press. 1992, pp. 255 and 258.

in real life. This convergence of the mother and nation, as conceived by the early nationalists, was more than a metaphor. It had the power of experienced reality.

Tagore was a part of the fashioning of this idea of nation as mother. But in his creativity, the idea acquired a new salience and poignancy in his famous novel *Gora* written between 1907 and 1910. The protagonist, after whom the novel is named, is a young man exceedingly proud and conscious of his Brahminical heritage and is committed to serving his motherland. He begins to work among downtrodden rural people. He is impatient and intolerant of ideas that aim to reform Hindu society. As he faced the harsh realities of the rural world where the poor were helpless and hopeless, he became disillusioned with the functioning of traditional Hindu society. Gora could not help but see that 'the armoury of rituals and customs was sucking the blood out of these people and cruelly leaving them without any rights.'[53] The novel takes an unexpected turn towards the end where Krishnadayal and Anandamayi, the couple that Gora knew to be his parents, reveal to him the unusual story of his birth. He was born of Irish parents in 1857 in Etawah during the

---

[53]Tagore describes Gora's disillusionment and reflections in chapter 67 of the novel in volume 6 of *Rabindra Rachanavali,* published in 15 volumes by the Government of West Bengal. The translation is mine.

great rebellion that engulfed North India in the summer of that year. Gora's biological father had been killed by the rebels. His mother, heavily pregnant, had taken refuge with Anandamayi and had died giving birth to Gora. Since then, Anandamayi had been Gora's mother, bringing him up as her own son. This revelation transforms Gora. He turns to Anandamayi in the epilogue of the novel and tells her, 'Ma, you are my Ma. The mother I was looking for everywhere was always here in my home. You have no caste, you do not discriminate and you have no hatred—you are the embodiment of goodness. You are my Bharatvarsha.'[54] The convergence of mother and the nation is here complete; moreover, the mother is a physical presence, not an imaginary one. Gora's cry from his heart to his mother, 'You have no caste, you do not discriminate and you have no hatred—you are the embodiment of goodness,' appears as a summation of Tagore's idea of India which is echoed in parts of 'Jana Gana Mana'.

In 'Jana Gana Mana', Tagore brings in a twist to what was a common theme in nationalist literature. In the song, the mother is not the nation/country. She is the divine dispenser of India's destiny, that Eternal

---

[54]Ibid., Chapter 76.

Being who is the driver/charioteer of India's past, present, and future. Divinity now has a gender. This is not just a dramatic turn in the then prevalent discourse of Indian nationalism but also in Tagore's own idea of piety. Tutored by his father, Debendranath, active in the Brahmo Samaj and immersed in his own reading and understanding of the Upanishads, Tagore's devotions had been focused on nirakara iswara (attributeless divinity). But in the song, he gives to the Eternal Being, in quite an emphatic manner, a female identity. Orthodox Hindu beliefs to which Tagore did not subscribe would see in the female identity a celebration of the goddess Shakti. This is an apparent contradiction here that Tagore did not resolve. To sing in praise of the nation/country as mother was one thing, perhaps only an evocative rhetorical artifice, but to see divinity as having female form marked for Tagore a theological displacement.

Some of the themes and motifs that occur in 'Jana Gana Mana' were derived from earlier musical compositions. For example, the reiteration of 'Jaye hey' (victory) as a refrain echoes a song Tagore had sung on 10 January 1891 at a reception for the volunteers who had worked to organize in Calcutta the sixth session of the Indian National Congress in late December 1890. This song, which had been written by one of Tagore's elder brothers, Satyendranath, had the lines, 'Jai Bharater jai, gao Bharater Jai' (victory to Bharat, victory, sing victory to Bharat).[55] A second notable influence was a song, 'Namo Hindustani' composed by his niece, Sarala Devi.[56] The song, as the name reveals, was in salutation of Hindustan in contrast to Tagore's use of Bharat, but the song mentioned the different regions—Banga, Bihar, Utkal, Madras, Maratha, Gujarat, Punjab, and Rajasthan. It went to add the different religious communities— Hindus, Parsis, Jains, Christians, Sikhs, and Muslims (to these Tagore was to add Buddhists), and urged them all to offer their worship to Hindustan (Namo Hindustan) and hail its victory (jai, victory, being repeated three times). These influences on 'Jana Gana Mana' are too obvious to be laboured.

The ideas embedded in 'Jana Gana Mana' were located within a particular context of Tagore's creative sensibilities and his evolving views about the nature and features of India's history and civilization. He had seen the harsh and stark realities of Bengal's rural world, what in *Gora* he called 'this vast, withdrawn rural world—how isolated,

---

[55]Prasantakumar Pal, *Rabijibani*, Vol. 3, Calcutta: Ananda Publishers, 1987, p. 164.
[56]The first verse of this song is available in Sen, *Bharatvarsher Jatiya Sangeet*, p. 40.

how constricted, how enfeebled...[where] the burden of inert ignorance and suffering, vast and terrifying, weighs upon the shoulders of all of us, learned and unlearned, rich and poor.'[57] He had been active in the Swadeshi Movement to protest against oppressive and divisive policies of the British rulers. This experience of activism in politics left him dissatisfied, if not disillusioned. Some of his poems, written in this period and in the wake of the Swadeshi Movement, suggest he was withdrawing from and renouncing the real world for the world of spirituality. This is to simplify. Tagore never renounced the reality around him. There is evidence of this not only in his writings of this period but also in his activities and the projects he initiated especially in education and agriculture.[58] This period, informed as it was by profound reflection on several critical issues, helped in his arriving at a view on India's history and civilization. There are many pieces, written during this period (1910–12), in which he articulated this view with clarity and power. I am taking only three examples since they seem to me

---

[57] *Gora*, Chapter 26. The translation is by Sukanta Chaudhuri and is taken from his translation of Sankha Ghosh's essay referred to in the next footnote.

[58] This point is very persuasively argued by Sankha Ghosh, 'Rabindranath Tagore: from Art to Life' in Chaudhuri (ed.), *The Cambridge Companion to Rabindranath Tagore*, pp. 1–11.

to be of some relevance to understanding 'Jana Gana Mana'. One comes, almost predictably from *Gora*. After he has learnt about his origin, Gora rushes to the house of Pareshbabu, the calm and devout Brahmo, with whom Gora had always argued and declares to him, 'Today, I am liberated...Today I am an Indian. Today within me there is no conflict with anyone—Hindus, Muslims, Christians. Every caste in India is my caste, everyone's food is my food...Imbibe in me the *mantra* of that God who belongs to everybody—Hindus, Muslims, Christians, Brahmo to all...who is not the God of only the Hindus but is the God of Bharatvarsha.'[59]

Tagore expressed the same idea in poetic terms in 'Bharat Tirtha' (Pilgrimage of India) written in 1910, which he included in *Gitanjali*. The poem deserves to be quoted in full:

> O my soul, on this sacred soil awaken tranquilly
> Here, upon India's ocean-shore of great humanity.
>> In worship of the human god
>> My two hands here I raise:
>> In measures free, with ecstasy
>> I sing his song of praise

---

[59] *Gora*, Chapter 76. The translation is mine.

These solemn meditating peaks,
These rivers, rows of prayer-beads
Clasped by the plains—the sacred earth
Here you may ever see
On India's ocean-shore of great humanity.

No one knows at whose great call
      Streams of humanity
In a mighty tide flowed who knows whence
      To mingle in that sea.
Aryan and non-Aryan came,
      Chinese, Dravidian
Scythian, Hun, Mughal, Pathan,
      In body blent as one:
And now the West unfolds its doors,
The world bears bounty from its store—
Give and receive, merge and be merged:
      None will excluded be

From India's ocean-shore of great humanity.

On battle's tide, with clamour wild,
      All those who came in throngs
Through desert and through mountain pass,

Singing their victory songs,
Within me they all dwell today:
   Not one is alien.
Along my blood their music plays
   In varied unison.
Play on, play on, O veena fierce:
Those who stand far off, still averse,
Will break their bonds, they too will gather
   Round in amity
On India's ocean-shore of great humanity.

Here once arose without a pause
   The mighty sound of Om—
The heart-strings resonated
   With the anthem of the One.
The many being sacrificed
   To the One's holy fire,
Division lost, one great soul rose
   By contemplation's power.
Today that sacrificial hall
Of worship and essay of soul
Is open: all must mingle there,
   Bound in humility
On India's ocean-shore of great humanity.

That holy fire blazes still
    With sorrow's blood-red flames—
It must be borne, burning at heart:
    So destiny ordains.
My soul, O bear this suffering,
    Hear the call of the One:
Conquer all shame, conquer all fear,
    Banish opprobrium
Once past the intolerable pain,
What vast life will be born again—
The night's at end, the Mother wakes
    In her nest's immensity
On India's ocean-shore of great humanity.

Aryan and non-Aryan come,
    Hindu and Musulman:
Come, O Christian; and today
    Come, O you Englishman.
Come, brahman, with a heart made pure
    Hold hands with one and all:
Come, you outcaste: let your load
    Of insult from you fall.
To the mother's coronation haste:
The sacred pitcher yet awaits
Its holy water, by the touch

Of all lent sanctity
On India's ocean-shore of great humanity.[60]

Tagore's view of India's history and his understanding
of what he thought was at the very core of Indian
civilization was presented in a cluster of essays. In
these he argued that in spite of the presence of many
people and many cultures over the ages in India, there
had been a unifying force at work. The differences had
not been ironed out but had been fused. In one essay
he wrote, 'Bharatvarsha has attempted the bonding
of dissimilars. Where there is genuine difference, it is
possible to accommodate it in its appropriate place and
thereby bring it within the unity. You cannot legislate
unity into existence.' The characteristic feature of
Indian civilization has been the quest to find unity
amidst a plurality of cultures. Reiterating the point
he wrote, 'India has always sought one thing only:
to establish unity in diversity, to direct many paths
towards the same goal, to perceive the one among the
many indubitably and profoundly—to secure
the intrinsic affinity without destroying external

---

[60]This translation is by Sukanta Chaudhuri and is taken from Chaudhuri
(ed.), *Rabindranath Tagore*. This translation is also available in Rudrangshu
Mukherjee, *The Best of Tagore*.

differences.'[61] He contrasted this with the West's attempts to obliterate differences through imperialist domination.

Writing on the reconciliation of opposites which he considered to be the essence of India's history and culture, Tagore, in another essay, noted, 'Where the harmony between the component differences has been organically effected, there beauty has blossomed; so long as it remains wanting, there is no end to deformities.' Tagore admitted that the search of harmony had not been perfect and without barriers. This quest for unity was not confined only to elites and upper castes. Tagore wrote that in one era of India's history, '...the message of the spiritual freedom and unity of man mainly sprang from the obscure strata of the community, where belonged the castes that were despised. Though it has to be admitted that in the medieval age the Brahmin Ramananda was the first to give voice to the cry of unity, which is India's own, and in consequence lost his honoured privileges as a Brahmin guru, yet it is nonetheless true that most of our great saints of that time, who took up this cry in their life and teaching

---

[61]Both quotations are from 'Bharatvarsher Itihas', 1902, cited in Sabyasachi Bhattacharya, 'Tagore's View of History', *The Cambridge Companion to Tagore*, pp. 271–72.

and songs, came from the lower classes, one of them being a Muhammadan weaver, one a cobbler, and several coming from ranks of society whose touch would pollute the drinking water of the respectable section of Hindus.' This was an ancient quest: to seek 'goodness... in the truth of perfect union'. Tagore's prayer for India was taken from a verse of the Svetasvatara Upanishad: 'He who is one, who is above all colour distinctions, who dispenses the inherent needs of men of all colours, who comprehends all things from their beginning to the end, let Him unite us to one another with the wisdom which is the wisdom of goodness.'[62]

Many of the ideas presented above from Tagore's writings around 1910 and 1912, exactly the period when he composed 'Jana Gana Mana', are reflected in the song. The diversity and plurality of India—in terms of varied population, in terms of geography and regional variations, in terms of the different faiths and cultures of the people who inhabit the space called Bharat. Beneath this surface diversity, there has always worked the force

---

[62]All quotations in this paragraph are from Tagore's essay, 'A Vision of India's History', which was a revised English rendering of a Bengali essay 'Bharatbarsher Itihaser Dhara' written in 1912. The English version came out in 1923. See, Das, *The English Writings of Tagore*, Vol. 3, 1994. The essay is reprinted in Mukherjee, *The Best of Tagore*, pp. 519, 521, and 524.

of unity. In the song, Tagore identified this force as the dispenser of India's destiny—Bharata bhagya bidhata around whose throne all, irrespective of their differences, gathered to weave the necklace of love. To borrow from Gora's plea to Pareshbabu, this was the God of India who bequeathed the mantra of unity and harmony. Tagore saw Bharat as a civilizational site to which many had come to 'merge and to be merged'. This is why, for him, India was a pilgrimage—a site to come to with heads bowed and 'bound in humility'. Bharat was not a place for the display of arrogance. Unity was anchored in compassion. This is why Tagore loved India. 'I love India,' he wrote, 'not because I cultivate the idolatry of geography, not because I have had the chance to be born in her soil, but because she has saved through tumultuous ages the living words that have issued from the illuminated consciousness of her great sons: Satyam, Jnanam, Anantam Brahma, Brahma is truth, Brahma is wisdom, Brahma is infinite; Santam, Sivam, Advaitam, peace is Brahma, goodness is in Brahma, and the unity of all beings.'[63] 'Jana Gana Mana' celebrates this unity and the maker of this unity—'Thou bringest the hearts of all peoples into the harmony of one life.'

---

[63]Ibid., p. 524.

In the poem, 'Pilgrimage to India', there is the admission that the promise of unity is not complete— 'The sacred pitcher yet awaits/its holy water'. The incompleteness contains the responsibility to forge ahead. This idea of a future is reflected in 'Jana Gana Mana', albeit in a slightly different way: 'The night dawns, the sun rises in the East...India wakes up.' There could, of course, be a literal reading of the line 'the sun rises in the East'—it does every day with regularity. But perhaps, Tagore is suggesting something transcending the diurnal. Was he suggesting that an India just waking up was the site of an entirely new kind of civilization? One draws courage to even frame such a question from Tagore's essay 'Crisis in Civilization', written in Bengali in April 1941, four months before his death, when civilization as it had existed had shrivelled through violence, death, and devastation. Towards the end of the essay Tagore wrote, 'As I look around, I see the crumbling ruins of a proud civilization strewn like a vast heap of futility. And yet I shall not commit the grievous sin of losing faith in Man. I would rather look forward to the opening of a new chapter in his history after the cataclysm is over and the atmosphere rendered clean with the spirit of service and sacrifice. Perhaps that dawn will come from this horizon, from the East where the sun rises.'[64]

The idea of a dawn from 'this horizon, from the East' was already there in embryo in the song of India—'Jana Gana Mana'.

---

[64]The text of this address is available, amongst other places, in Mukherjee, *The Best of Tagore*, pp. 643–49.

NOTES OF DISSONANCE

Nehru recollected in Tagore's centenary year that he had requested the latter, a little before his death, to compose a national anthem for a new India. The poet had partly agreed. What is very significant about this request and the response is that neither Nehru nor Tagore had thought of 'Jana Gana Mana' as the national anthem. Nehru recollected very explicitly that when he had requested Tagore, he did not have 'Jana Gana Mana' in mind. He was obviously thinking of a new song. So was Tagore, since he did not suggest 'Jana Gana Mana'. It would not be entirely unjustified to aver that at this point of time—the last time Tagore and Nehru met—'Jana Gana Mana' was not their first choice as the national anthem of India. After Independence when Tagore was no longer alive the decision to make 'Jana Gana Mana' the national anthem was probably inspired by the choice that Subhas Chandra Bose had already made in the early 1940s.

It is worth posing the question, even at the risk of

speculation, why Tagore did not immediately suggest to Nehru that 'Jana Gana Mana' be made the national anthem. One possible answer is that Tagore possibly did not see 'Jana Gana Mana' as a song that upheld nationalism. The song was, of course, about India—its geography, its people, its religious faiths, and its unity. But it was more importantly a paean to the dispenser of India's destiny, Bharata bhagya bidhata. The stirring refrain 'Jaye hey' is to that bidhata. In this sense, the song is a hymn to divinity. It will be recalled that when Tagore published the text of the song in January 1912 on the pages of *Tattvabodhini Patrika* he described it as Brahmo sangeet.[65] If Tagore had lived longer and had acquiesced completely to Nehru's plea, it is possible that he would have composed a song on a different emotional register. It is possible to speculate this because from around the second decade of the twentieth century, Tagore's views on nationalism had undergone a radical transformation. He had been arguing in a series of essays and speeches across the world that nationalism was too restrictive, too inadequate—even corrosive—ideology and emotion. His thinking had veered towards a comprehensive humanism

---

[65]It should be noted that in the collection *Gitabitan* published in Tagore's lifetime, 'Jana Gana Mana' was placed under the rubric Swadesh.

which brought India and the world together. It is thus somewhat of an irony that one of his memorable songs clearly extolling divinity was made the anthem for the new nation state. The choice enriched India, but one is left with the lingering doubt that Tagore may not have completely approved. Nationalism in India appropriated a divine song.

Tagore's music drew from various sources. He could be, when he wanted, a purist, but equally true is his willingness to deviate from the purity of a raga. In spite of this musical eclecticism, one wonders what he would have made of a longish song being curtailed to only its first verse and then being played/sung for only fifty-two seconds to meet the protocol demands of a nation state.

'Jana Gana Mana' celebrates the unity of India and its people. But the song was made the national anthem only after the unity had been tragically shattered by an independence that came with the partition of the country. The song mentions Sindh as one of the regions of Bharat but when the song becomes the national anthem, Sindh was not a part of India that is Bharat. The unity that is hailed in the verses of the song had been adversely challenged when 'Jana Gana Mana' had been made into a national anthem.

Towards the end of the song, as has already been

noted, the dispenser of India's destiny is described as a tender and compassionate mother. In the course of 1946–47 and in the aftermath of Partition, indescribable violence destroyed the lives and homes of people. On the watch of the tender and compassionate mother, rape, murder, and plunder ripped apart the unity of India. Tagore's vision—idealization if you like—of India had been turned on its head. The words of the song could not but have a hollow ring to the victims of the partition holocaust. It could be argued that precisely when the unity had been ruptured, the unity had to be reiterated through an anthem. The bore of that violence took with it one of Tagore's closest associates, Mohandas Karamchand Gandhi, who had described 'Jana Gana Mana' as 'not only a song but...also like a devotional hymn'.[66]

'Jana Gana Mana', perhaps because it sprang from the fountainhead of Tagore's piety, had embedded in it the idea of destiny controlled by an eternal and supreme entity. Every phase of India's history and civilization carried the imprimatur of this divine will. It was possibly in this spirit that Nehru had unforgettably spoken of India's Independence as a 'tryst with destiny'. Stretching this notion of destiny, would it be unfair to argue that

---

[66]K. G. Mashruwala (ed.), *Harijan*, Vol. 10, No. 15.

Partition and the violence that was part of it were the outcome of the will of the dispenser of India's destiny? Did Bharata bhagya bidhata will it this way? Or should one leave the poet's lofty vision free from the messy ways in which human beings make their own history? However, there is some discord between a sense of destiny and the emphasis on human agency articulated in the statement 'We the people of India having solemnly resolved...', which opens the Preamble to the Constitution of India.

In spite of these notes of dissonance, 'Jana Gana Mana' remains unsurpassed as the song of India. Occasionally, in the course of the history of independent India some challengers have emerged. The most important of these has been 'Vande Mataram' (as noted earlier, a poem by Bankim Chandra, put to music by Tagore) which from the 1890s became the song of the nationalists and the rallying cry of all Indian nationalists. Rajendra Prasad in his statement to the Constituent Assembly regarding the national anthem (already referred to in the previous chapter) acknowledged the important role that 'Vande Mataram' had played in the national movement: '...the song Vande Mataram,' he said, 'which has played a historic part in the struggle for Indian freedom shall be honoured equally with 'Jana Gana Mana' and shall have equal status with it.' Nehru in his statement on the national anthem in the Constituent Assembly (again referred to in the previous chapter) noted that the then (1948) premier of West Bengal had informed the Constituent Assembly that he and his government preferred 'Vande Mataram'. Other than this, 'Jana Gana Mana' had no serious contenders to be the national anthem. Perhaps what tilted the balance in favour of 'Jana Gana Mana' was its extolling of Bharat in contrast to Vande Mataram's praise of Bengal. There was also the canard that the song had been written for the British emperor George V. That is nothing more than a canard, not deserving any further comment.

India's national anthem evokes a vision of India as perceived by a poet. The vision contains within it a promise and a pledge. Citizens when they stand up in respect when 'Jana Gana Mana' is played or sung should remember that standing to attention carries with it the responsibility to fulfil the promise and honour the pledge and thus fuse together the will of Bharata bhagya bidhata and the will and resolve of we the people of India.

CODA

The Morning Song of India

Thou art the ruler of the minds of all people, dispenser of India's destiny.
Thy name rouses the hearts of the Punjab, Sind, Gujrat and Maratha, of Dravid
and Orissa and Bengal; it echoes in the hills of the Vindhyas and Himalayas,
mingles in the music of the Ganges and the Jamuna and is chanted by the
surging waves of the Indian Sea. They pray for thy blessings and sing thy praise,
the saving of all people waits in thy hand, thou dispenser of India's destiny.
Victory, victory, victory to thee.

Day and night thy voice goes out from land to land calling the Hindus,
Buddhists, Sikhs and Jains round thy throne and the Parsees, Mussalmans and
Christians. The East and the West join hands in their prayer to thee, and the
garland of love is woven. Thou bringest the hearts of all people into the harmony
of one life, thou dispenser of India's destiny.
Victory, victory, victory to thee.

The procession of pilgrims passes over the endless road rugged with the
rise and fall of nations, and it resounds with the thunder of thy wheels,
Eternal Charioteer! Through the dire days of doom thy trumpet sounds and
men are led by thee across death. Thy finger points the path to all people.
Oh dispenser of India's destiny!
Victory, victory, victory to thee!

The darkness was dense and deep was the night. My country lay in a deathlike
silence of swoon. But thy mother-arms were round her and thine eyes gazed
upon her troubled face in sleepless love through her hours of ghastly dreams.
Thou art the companion and the saviour of the people in their sorrows, thou
dispenser of India's destiny.
Victory, victory, victory to thee!

The night fades; the light breaks over the peaks of the eastern hills; the
birds begin to sing and the morning breeze carries the breath of new life.
The rays of thy mercy have touched the waking land with their blessings.
Victory to thee, King of kings, victory to thee, the dispenser of India's destiny.
Victory, victory, victory to thee.

Rabindranath Tagore

Feb. 28. 1919

Courtesy : The Theosophical College, Madanapalle.

'The Morning Song of India' in Rabindranath Tagore's handwriting

জনগণমন-অধিনায়ক জয় হে, ভারতভাগ্যবিধাতা।
পঞ্জাব সিন্ধু গুজরাট মরাঠা দ্রাবিড় উৎকল বঙ্গ
বিন্ধ্য হিমাচল যমুনা গঙ্গা উচ্ছল জলধিতরঙ্গ
     তব শুভ নামে জাগে,   তব শুভ আশিস মাগে,
       গাহে তব জয়গাথা।
জনগণমঙ্গলদায়ক জয় হে, ভারতভাগ্যবিধাতা।
     জয় হে, জয় হে, জয় হে, জয় জয় জয়, জয় হে ॥

অহরহ তব আহ্বান প্রচারিত, শুনি তব উদার বাণী
হিন্দু বৌদ্ধ শিখ জৈন পারসিক মুসলমান খ্রীস্টানী
     পূরব পশ্চিম আসে   তব সিংহাসন-পাশে,
       প্রেমহার হয় গাঁথা।
জনগণ-ঐক্যবিধায়ক জয় হে, ভারতভাগ্যবিধাতা।
     জয় হে, জয় হে, জয় হে, জয় জয় জয়, জয় হে ॥

পতন-অভ্যুদয়-বন্ধুর পন্থা, যুগযুগধাবিত যাত্রী,
হে চিরসারথি, তব রথচক্রে মুখরিত পথ দিনরাত্রি।
     দারুণ বিপ্লব-মাঝে   তব শঙ্খধ্বনি বাজে
       সংকটদুঃখত্রাতা।
জনগণপথপরিচায়ক জয় হে, ভারতভাগ্যবিধাতা।
     জয় হে, জয় হে, জয় হে, জয় জয় জয়, জয় হে ॥

জাগ্রত ছিল তব আবচল মঙ্গল নতনয়নে আনমেষে।
দুঃস্বপ্নে আতঙ্কে   রক্ষা করিলে অঙ্কে
স্নেহময়ী তুমি মাতা।
জনগণদুঃখত্রায়ক জয় হে, ভারতভাগ্যবিধাতা।
জয় হে, জয় হে, জয় হে, জয় জয় জয়, জয় হে ॥

রাত্রি প্রভাতিল, উদিল রবিচ্ছবি পূর্ব উদয়গিরিভালে,
গাহে বিহঙ্গম, পুণ্য সমীরণ নবজীবনরস ঢালে।
তব করুণারুণরাগে   নিদ্রিত ভারত জাগে
তব চরণে নত মাথা।
জয় জয় জয় হে, জয় রাজেশ্বর, ভারতভাগ্যবিধাতা।
জয় হে, জয় হে, জয় হে, জয় জয় জয়, জয় হে ॥

'Jana Gana Mana' in the Bengali script

जनगणमन-अधिनायक

जनगणमन-अधिनायक जय हे भारतभाग्यविधाता।
पंजाब सिंधु गुजराट मराठा द्राविड़ उत्कल बंग
विंध्य हिमाचल यमुना गंगा उच्छलजलधितरंग
तव शुभ नामे जागे, तव शुभ आशिस मागे,
गाहे तव जयगाथा ।
जनगणमंगलदायक जय हे भारतभाग्यविधाता ।
जय हे, जय हे, जय हे, जय जय जय, जय हे ।।

अहरह तव आह्वान प्रचारित, शुनि तव उदार वाणी
हिन्दु बौद्ध सिख जैन पारसिक मुसलमान ख्रृष्टानी
पूरब-पश्चिम आसे तव सिंहासन-पाशे,
प्रेमहार हय गाँथा ।
जनगण-ऐक्यविधायक जय हे भारतभाग्यविधाता ।
जय हे, जय हे, जय हे, जय जय जय, जय हे ।।

पतन-अभ्युदय-बंधुर पन्था, युगयुगधावित यात्री,
हे चिरसारथि, तव रथचक्रे मुखरित पथ दिनरात्रि ।
दारूण-विप्लव-माझे तव शंखध्वनि बाजे,
संकटदुःखत्राता ।
जनगणपथपरिचायक जय हे भारतभाग्यविधाता ।
जय हे, जय हे, जय हे, जय जय जय, जय हे ।।

घोर तिमिरघन निविड़ निशीथे पीड़ित मूर्छित देशे
जाग्रत छिल तव अविचल नंगल नतनयने अनिमेषे
दुःस्वप्ने आतंके रक्षा करिले अंके
स्नेहमयी तुमि माता ।
जन गण दुःखत्रायक जय हे भारत भाग्य विधाता ।
जय हे जय हे जय हे, जय जय जय जय हे ।।

रात्रि प्रभातिल, उदिल रविच्छवि पूर्व–उदयगिरिभाले
गाहे विहंगम, पुण्य समीरण नवजीवनरस ढाले
तव करुणारुणरागे निद्रित भारत जागे
तव चरणे नत माथा ।
जय जय जय हे जय राजेश्वर भारत भाग्य विधाता ।
जय हे जय हे जय हे, जय जय जय जय हे ।।

'Jana Gana Mana' in the Devanagari script

Jana-Gana-Mana-Adhinayaka

I

Jana-gaṇa-mana-adhināyaka, jaya hē Bhārata-bhāgya-
vidhātā.

Panjāba-Sindhu-Gujarāṭa-Marāṭhā-Drāviḍa-Utkala-Vaṅga
Vindhya-Himāchala-Yamunā-Gaṅgā uchchhala-jaladhi-
taraṅga

Tava śubha nāmē jāgē, tava śubha āśisa māgē
gāhē tava jaya-gāthā.

Jana-gaṇa-maṅgala-dāyaka, jaya hē Bhārata-bhāgya-
vidhātā.

Jaya hē, jaya hē, jaya hē, jaya jaya jaya, jaya hē

II

Aharaha tava āhvāna prachārita, śuni tava udāra vāṇī
Hindu-Bauddha-Śikha-Jaina-Pārasika-Musalmāna-
Khristānī

Pūrava-paśchima āsē tava siṃhāsana-pāśē,
prēma-hāra haya gānthā.

Jana-gaṇa-aikya-vidhāyaka, jaya hē Bhārata-bhāgya-
vidhātā.

Jaya hē, jaya hē, jaya hē, jaya jaya jaya, jaya hē

III

Patana-abhyudaya-bandhura panthā, yuga-yuga-dhāvita
yātrī,

Hē chira-sārathi, tava ratha-chakrē mukharita patha dina-rātri.
Dāruṇa-viplava-mājhē tava śaṅkhadhvani bājē
saṅkata-duḥkhatrātā.
Jana-gaṇa-patha-parichāyaka, jaya hē Bhārata-bhāgya-
vidhātā.
Jaya hē, jaya hē, jaya hē, jaya jaya jaya, jaya hē

IV

Ghōra-timira-ghana-nivida-niśīthē pīḍita-mūrchhita dēśē
Jāgrata chhila tava avidhala maṅgala nata-nayanē animēṣē.
Duḥsvapnē ātaṅkē rakṣā karilē aṅkē,
snēhamayī tumi mātā.
Jana-gaṇa-duḥkhatrāyaka, jaya hē Bhārata-bhāgya-vidhātā.
Jaya hē, jaya hē, jaya hē, jaya jaya jaya, jaya hē

V

Rātri prabhātila, udila ravichchhavi pūrva-udaya-giri-
bhālē,
Gāhe vihaṅgama, puṇya samīraṇa nava-jīvana-rasa ḍhālē,
Tava karuṇāruṇa-rāgē nidrita Bhārata jāgē,
tava charaṇē nata māthā.
Jaya jaya jaya hē, jaya rājēśvara, Bhārata-bhāgya-vidhātā.
Jaya hē, jaya hē, jaya hē, jaya jaya jaya, jaya hē

A transliteration of 'Jana Gana Mana' in the Roman script

Thou Art the Ruler of the Minds of All People

Thou art the ruler of the minds of all people,
Thou Dispenser of India's destiny.
Thy name rouses the hearts
of the Punjab, Sind, Gujarat and Maratha,
of Dravida, Orissa and Bengal.
It echoes in the hills of the Vindhyas and Himalayas,
mingles in the music of Jumna and Ganges,
and is chanted by the waves of the Indian Sea.
They pray for thy blessing and sing thy praise,
Thou dispenser of India's destiny,
Victory, Victory, Victory to thee.

Day and night, thy voice goes out from land to land,
Calling Hindus, Buddhists, Sikhs and Jains round thy
throne
and Parsees, Mussalmans and Christians.
Offerings are brought to thy shrine by the East and
the West
to be woven in a garland of love.
Thou bringest the hearts of all peoples into the harmony
    of one life,
Thou Dispenser of India's destiny,
Victory, Victory, Victory to thee.

Eternal Charioteer, thou drivest man's history
along the road rugged with rises and falls of Nations.
Amidst all tribulations and terror
thy trumpet sounds to hearten those that despair
and droop,
and guide all people in their paths of peril and pilgrimage.
Thou Dispenser of India's destiny,
Victory, Victory, Victory to thee.

When the long dreary night was dense with gloom
and the country lay still in a stupor,
thy Mother's arms held her,
thy wakeful eyes bent upon her face,
till she was rescued from the dark evil dreams
that oppressed her spirit,
Thou Dispenser of India's destiny,
Victory, Victory, Victory to thee.

The night dawns, the sun rises in the East,
the birds sing, the morning breeze brings a stir of
     new life.
Touched by golden rays of thy love
India wakes up and bends her head at thy feet.
Thou King of all Kings,
Thou Dispenser of India's destiny,
Victory, Victory, Victory to thee.

The English translation of 'Jana Gana Mana'

Jana Gana Mana

RABINDRANATH TAGORE

Sheet music of 'Jana Gana Mana'

Scan the QR code to listen to Rabindranath
Tagore's rendition of 'Jana Gana Mana'.

SELECT BIBLIOGRAPHY

Bose, Sugata, *The Nation as Mother and Other Visions of Nationhood*, New Delhi: Viking, 2017.

Chaudhuri, Sukanta (ed.), *The Cambridge Companion to Rabindranath Tagore*, Cambridge: Cambridge University Press, 2020.

———— *Rabindranath Tagore: Selected Poems*, Oxford Tagore Translations, New Delhi: Oxford University Press, 2004.

Constituent Assembly Debates [online facsimile].

Das, Sisir Kumar (ed.), *The English Writings of Rabindranath Tagore*, New Delhi: Sahitya Akademi, 1994.

Dutta, Krishna and Robinson, Andrew, *Rabindranath Tagore: The Myriad-Minded Man*, New York: St Martin's Press, 1995.

Ghosh, Nityapriya, *The English Writings of Rabindranath Tagore*, Vol. 4, New Delhi: Sahitya Akademi, 2007.

Mukherjee, Rudrangshu, 'The Last Testament', *Seminar*, No. 623, July 2011.

————— *Tagore and Gandhi: Walking Alone, Walking Together*, New Delhi: Aleph Book Company, 2021.

————— (ed.), *The Best of Tagore*, London: Everyman's Library, 2023.

Mukhopadhyay, Prabhat Kumar, *Rabindra Jibani*, in 4 vols, Kolkata: Visva Bharati, several reprints.

Prasantakumar Pal, *Rabijibani*, 9 volumes, Calcutta: Ananda Publishers, 1982–2003.

Rabindra Rachanavali, 15 volumes, Calcutta: Government of West Bengal.

Rabindra Rachanavali, 18 volumes, Calcutta: Visva Bharati.

Ray, Satyajit, 'Portrait of a Man', *UNESCO Courier*, December 1961.

Sen, Prabodhchandra, *Bharatvarsher Jatiya Sangeet*, Calcutta: Purbasha, 1948.

————— *India's National Anthem*, Calcutta: Visva Bharati, 1949.

www.ingramcontent.com/pod-product-compliance
Lightning Source LLC
Chambersburg PA
CBHW020441100426
42812CB00036B/3403/J